THE FLYING ARTIST'S GUIDE TO

SKETCHING

BARNES
& NOBLE
BOOKS

NEW YORK

This edition published by Barnes & Noble, Inc.
by Arrangement with Spicebox™
2005 Barnes & Noble Books

Copyright © Spicebox™ 2005
Text Copyright © Philip Berrill 1996
Written and Illustrated by Philip Berrill

M 10 9 8 7 6 5 4 3 2 1
ISBN 0-7607-7149-9

Printed in China

CONTENTS

THE FLYING ARTIST'S GUIDE TO SKETCHING CONTAINS 25 DEMONSTRATIONS FOR YOU TO TRY.

Philip Berrill
"The Flying Artist"

Philip Berril is a professional artist, art tutor, lecturer and author whose techniques and methods of learning to paint are taught and enjoyed worldwide. Born in 1945 in Northampton, England, Philip now lives in Southport with his wife Sylvia and daughter Penelope. When asked how he first embarked on his career path, Philip recalls the tale of how he discovered paint at the age of three. It was one sunny afternoon that Philip wandered into his father's glass greenhouse in their backyard and saw at the far end a large bucket of whitewash and a tubular pump sprayer. Being naturally inquisitive, Philip loaded the sprayer with whitewash from the bucket and had a lovely afternoon spraying all his father's best tomatoes and plants white. By the time his father returned to find his son and the entire inside of the greenhouse dripping with whitewash, Philip had discovered that with paint you could change the world.

By the age of 14, Philip's enjoyment of art at school, where he studied under the Welsh artist and tutor, John Sullivan, helped him decide to make a living as a professional artist. Philip held his first one-man exhibition at the age of 18 followed by other group and one-man exhibitions. At the age of 28 a major exhibition of his work was held at Liverpool University and as a direct result of this exhibition Philip realized his ambition to become established as a professional artist. He launched his very successful art classes using his special approach to teaching, sketching and painting. These classes proved so popular Philip went on to develop his worldwide correspondence art courses. In the 1980s Philip embarked on the next stage of his career that lead to his nickname "The Flying Artist". After offering highly sought-after painting holiday courses in Great Britain, additional tutoring and painting holidays in Europe were then organized in wonderful locations such as Rome, Venice, Florence and Paris. Subsequently Philip was invited to lecture and demonstrate painting on sea cruises around Europe and visits followed to Houston, Dallas and Dubai. Philips exhibition "The Italian Connection", an exhibition of his sketches and paintings of his Italian journeys and other European locations, has been very well received.

Philip's love and enthusiasm for sketching and painting is infectious. He believes that art should be for everyone and that you are never too young or too old to start sketching. Philip's students have ranged from 10 to 80 years of age and he continues to enjoy passing on his enthusiasm and knowledge of how to sketch and paint, gained over 30 years, to people from all walks of life and almost every background imaginable. Philip's sketching and painting courses and techniques are designed to be suitable for people of all abilities and all ages, and he has over recent years found great enjoyment in the challenge of producing his

Left: Philip Berrill demonstrating painting to the public at a recent Beijing Book Fair.

own art videos. These videos led to the invitation to produce and present his own 13 part television series, "Paint with the Flying Artist" and this project in turn has led to the writing and illustrating of his own series of art books especially for you. These books, "The Flying Artist's Guide to..." are designed to cover a wide range of mediums, techniques and subjects to introduce you to the joy and pleasure of sketching and painting. Each book has been beautifully presented in a high quality laptop easel with all the materials you will need to get started painting and drawing. The compact form and portability of each kit will allow you the freedom and spontaneity to capture each moment of inspiration the way Philip demonstrates with his own work.

We hope that you will enjoy the "Flying Artist's Guide to..." kits and that they will assist you in your journey of sketching and painting.

Below. Philip was painting one day in Venice. A film crew appeared and started to record a television commercial close by. The model, the car and the wonderful Venetian backdrop presented a new subject. Philip broke off from the scene he was painting and using pen and wash quickly sketched this unique subject.

Above: Philip Berrill sketching a statue.

Introduction to Sketching by Philip Berrill

What is "A B S"?

"A B S" Always Be Sketching, is a favourite saying of mine. If you have ever said "I wish I could paint, but I can't draw a straight line", then sketching could be the first step to introducing you to the marvelous world of art.

Why Sketch?

Not only can sketching be fun in its own right, it is also quite simply the key to creating successful paintings. Experience has taught me that many people who already paint greatly underestimate the value of sketching, when in fact it is the most economical introduction to learning the essentials of picture making. Most of the great masters were great sketchers and if they found sketching important and worthwhile, we should take sketching equally seriously. Whether you are a newcomer to painting or you are at a more advanced stage, I invite you to join with me to read and sketch your way through this book and discover the delights sketching can offer you.

What is a Sketch?

It is important to spend a few moments thinking about exactly what a sketch is. What does it set out to achieve? How much information is included in a sketch? Can you sketch in different mediums? Is a sketch just made in black and white or can you sketch in color? What is the difference between a sketch and a drawing?

A sketch is a versatile way to express ideas and to put down on paper the initial visual information about a subject. The subject can be real, from a photograph, inspired by poetry, prose or music, or from your imagination. The sketch is often the first exploratory stage for a painting. It can be part of the preparation, which may include one or more sketches, to explore, play with and develop an idea or subject into a foundation for a finished drawing or painting. Sketches should be flexible in that they can be altered, changed and adapted. Sometimes a sketch is just a few fleeting lines that capture the essentials of the subject. At other times a sketch may contain more information, including details on light and shade, textures and color notes. When you do not have time to paint a picture of an eye-catching view you can make a quick sketch and take a photograph of it. The sketch and photograph will allow you to paint a picture of the view at home or in your studio.

Anything that makes a mark can be used to sketch with. The great joy of sketching is that you can start with a humble pencil on the back of an envelope; you do not need fancy equipment or expensive paper. Many sketches have spontaneity and freshness that can be difficult to capture in a finished painting. This is often because when first painting, people try too hard to get the painting just right, whereas one is more relaxed when sketching and less worried about making mistakes. This same spontaneity in a painting comes from speed; the speed comes from experience and the experience from practice. Sketching is a wonderful form of practice.

Also, don't confuse sketching with drawing. A sketch can contain as little or as much information as you feel is necessary. Conversely, in a drawing, the subject, content and composition and style have been decided on by the artist. A sketch tends to be looser, more exploratory and sometimes incomplete. However, many a sketch will stand as an attractive, keepable, frameable and saleable work of art in its own right. Sketching is essentially the visual expression of ideas about real or imaginary subjects. Let your sketching be fun!

Right. Black and white on a gray background sketches can be very expressive.

Below. A selection of sketches from Philip's portfolio

7

Materials for Sketching

Let's Get Started

Almost anything that can make a mark can be used to sketch with. The early cave painters of France and Spain produced the most dramatic of images with very basic materials that were found around them in their own environment. There was no prehistoric art shop along the road in which to buy art supplies, they had to improvise in the creation of their own sketching and painting materials. There were no art teachers to help them, yet they produced stunning pictures based on their own life and experiences as a means of communicating their images and thoughts to their fellow cave dwellers. We are fortunate to have a superb selection of art materials conveniently available from art shops at affordable prices. The materials we buy and use today have been made based on the knowledge, skills, experience and needs of artists, and from their desire to create images over the centuries.

All you need to start sketching is a pencil and a sheet of paper. If you look around your home you will be able to find many other suitable materials for sketching, including ballpoint pens, pencils, fountain pens, felt-tipped and nylon-tipped pens, colored pens and plain copy paper or writing paper. It is possible to sketch in a wide range of other mediums including colored pencils, water colors, pastels and oil paints. We will look at these techniques using color in later stages in this book.

Pencils

Conté are amongst the leaders in the manufacturing of pencils and sketching materials for artists. Pencils are made from a mixture of graphite and china clay. The more graphite there is in the pencil the softer it is, and the darker the mark it will make. The more china clay in the mixture the harder the pencil, and the sharper, less dark the line, or mark, it will make. The pencil lead is normally mounted in wood and is circular or hexagonal in shape. Soft pencils are known as B, harder pencils as H. They are also numbered 2,3,4,5,6,7,8 and 9. The higher the number, the softer, or harder, the pencil.

2B and 3B are medium soft and are ideal for sketching. 7,8 and 9 B are too soft and smudgy for general work, but do have their uses. The H pencils are too hard for most art work, being preferred for technical or engineering drawing. HB pencils are in everyday use for writing as they are an all purpose pencil, especially suitable for writing and note taking.

Carpenters' Pencils

These are made in a similar manner to the traditional round pencils but are rectangular in shape. They can be sharpened to a chisel-like end and offer a different variety of pencil marks compared to the normal pencil.

Graphite Sticks

These are sticks of graphite not bound in a wooden casing but varnished or wrapped in paper to stop the graphite dirtying your fingers. The main advantage to using a graphite stick is that you can use the tip as a normal pencil, but the wide side of the sharpened end can be used for bold sweeps of pencil marks and for the shading of large areas. Both carpenters' pencils and graphite sticks can be obtained in varying B degrees of softness.

Pens

Dip-in, sketching or mapping pens are the most common. These have a metallic nib in a wooden or plastic holder. The pen is dipped into ink to load the nib of the pen.

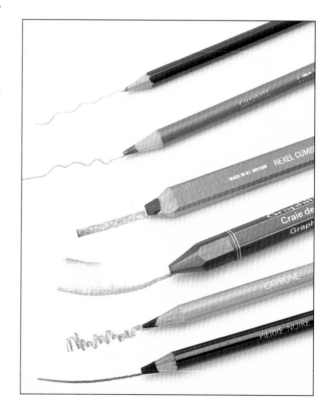

India and Colored Inks

India ink is black and lightfast (won't fade). It comes in waterproof and non-waterproof forms but I recommend the waterproof version for sketching. Colored inks are also available, but the main problem with them is that when exposed to normal daylight for any length of time they often fade. They are ideally suited to work that will not be exposed to a great deal of light.

Fountain Pens

The regular fountain pen can be used to sketch with as well. Some manufacturers have a range of fountain pens for sketching on the market. These use non-waterproof ink cartridges, not India ink. India ink contains a mild glue and can clog a fountain pen so be sure to use regular fountain pen ink. Use India ink only for dip-in pens or brush drawing work.

Ballpoint Pens

The domestic ballpoint pen is an ideal tool for quick sketching.

Felt-tip and Nylon-Tip Pens

The tremendous number, range of sizes and types of points on modern felt and synthetic-tip pens provide a bewildering choice for the artist. Experiment; find one or two pens you feel comfortable with. Some pens are waterproof, others are not. Most of the colored pens will fade in strong light. Ask your local art or stationery store to explain the qualities of the various pens they stock. Many have sample pens you can try out in the store.

Colored Pencils

Some colored pencils are water soluble, often known as aquarelle, others are not water soluble and are used just for applying dry color. Conté Aquarelle pencils can be used dry, or brushed over with a wash of water to create color-life effects. A set of Aquarelle pencils provides a variety of ways of using color in sketches.

Conté Carres: Crayons

These are square sticks of firm pastel. The most common colors are black, gray, white, sanguine and sepia. They offer beautiful results, especially on tinted paper.

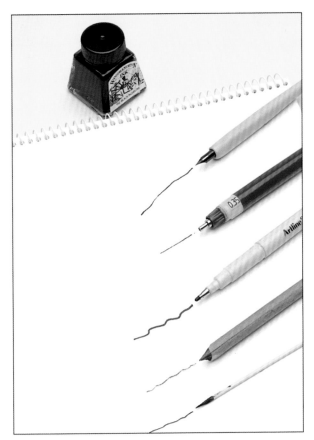

Sepia, Sanguine and White Conté Pastel Pencils

Similar to above, but in pencil format, these also offer exciting sketching opportunities on tinted paper.

Conté Carbon Graphic Pencil

This is designed for finer, more defined lines and is ideal for sketching and technical drawing.

Conté Pierre Noire

This sketching pencil is made from a filtered paste pigment and gives a deep, solid and indelible matte black every time.

Charcoal

Black, burnt wood. This is usually made from willow wood and is available in single sticks or boxed in thin, medium, thick or assorted sticks. Charcoal can be reduced to powder by the manufacturers, remixed and reformed into compressed sticks of charcoal in different pencil-like degrees of softness.

Erasers

A general, all purpose eraser is sufficient, but the one preferred by most artists is the kneadable rubber eraser because it can by molded with your fingers into all sorts of shapes for rubbing out, modifying and lifting out passages or work. Also, it does not create lots of loose pieces of paper and eraser so the work does not have to be dusted off by hand which in turns reduces the risk of smudging.

Fixative

Pencils, charcoal and Conté pastels need "fixing" to prevent them from smudging. Clear fixative is widely available in spray can form.

Paper

Cartridge paper is the most popular and can be obtained by the sheet, or in a pad which can be coil bound gummed. Popular sizes are 4" x 6" (100 mm x 150mm), 6" x 8" (150mm x 200mm), 9" x 12" (230mm x 305mm), 12" x 18" (305mm x 455mm), 14" x 17" (355mm x 430mm) and 18" x 24" (455mm x 610mm). Sketching paper can be obtained in different weights and thicknesses as well, but 80 lb (110g) paper is ideal for most sketching work.

Brushes

Round and flat, sable, or the modern synthetic hair brushes enable color to be used either directly, or in conjunction with another sketching medium. The

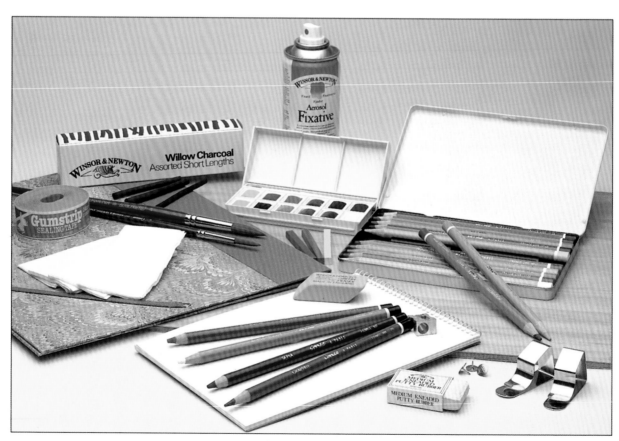

Winsor and Newton Cotman and Sceptre ranges are good value for money.

Pencil Sharpeners, Craft Knives and Sandpaper

You can use any of the above tools to bring your pencil point to the shape you would like to use for the sketch you plan to make.

Paints

A Winsor and Newton pocket set of Artist Quality, or Cotman water color fi pans will provide a compact set of paints for indoor and outdoor sketching.

Drawing Boards

The case of your Flying Artist Kit can be secured with the snaps on the side to create an easel to support your paper. You can also use a clipboard for smaller sketches, or a sturdy piece of cardboard for your larger work.

Drawing Pins, Drawing Board Clips, Masking Tape

Try not to use drawing pins as they make marks in the board which can show through in other work if shading or drawing over the holes. Drawing board clips will hold the paper to the board, but I usually secure my paper to the board with masking tape.

Tissues

Soft tissues are handy for wiping your pen nib or brush when sketching or painting.

Easels

An easel is not essential for sketching, however aside from your kit, table easels are available and many people enjoy working on them. The Winsor and Newton table easel adjusts to four angles of incline and folds flat when not in use. Metal or wooden sketching easels can be very useful indoors, but are especially useful on outdoor sketching trips.

Portfolio

A 9"x12" or 12" x 18" portfolio will keep your sketches clean and flat.

Table easel

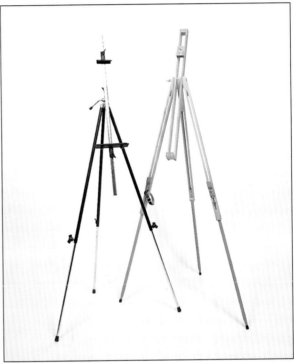

Sketching easels

Sketching materials

Sketching: Discover Your Style

There are almost as many styles of sketching as there are artists. Everyone's style of handwriting differs and so do styles of sketching. My own style is neat and tidy, but I have seen and equally enjoyed looking at very vigorous free flowing work by other artists. Look at pictures in art galleries, art publications and magazines and look at fine art prints in art stores to discover the very many and varied styles artists have used and continue to use. One artist may use a few quick lines to encapsulate the subject, another may use many lines. One artist may use little or no color, another could use vibrant colors in his or her interpretation of the same subject. You may be attracted by the style of one artist and not another, but think how boring it would be if all sketches and paintings looked the same! Explore your own natural style by trying subjects in different sketching mediums.

With the tree I used a 2B pencil for the pencil sketch, then I tried a monochrome sketch using a water soluble felt-tip pen and created a monochrome by brushing over it with a little water. Finally, I made a pen and wash sketch in color.

Pencil

A water soluble felt-tip pen brushed with water

Pen and Wash

12

Demonstration 1
Let's Get To The Point

The shape of the point of your pencil can make its own distinctive contribution to your sketch. While you can just pick up a pencil and sketch away, let's think about the pencil point. Do you want a sharp point giving a fine, sharp line or a more rounded point giving a different width of line? Would a less sharp point be of benefit to a particular sketch? The way you sharpen your pencil can make quite a difference to a sketch.

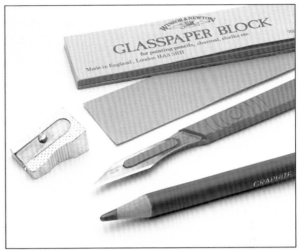

A fine sandpaper pad, craft knife or pencil sharpener can be used to sharpen a pencil lead

A pencil sharpener can be used to give a clear, sharp point to the pencil. But, by using a craft knife or penknife, you can vary the length of pencil lead exposed. Use the knife to slice away the wood around the pencil point. Do not try to shape the pencil lead with the knife. Always keep fingers behind cutting edges.

Sharpening with a knife

By rubbing the pencil point on a sheet of fine sandpaper you can make the tip more rounded, or create a chisel-like edge to the pencil tip. Try creating sharp, pointed, rounded and chisel ends to your pencil and compare the types of lines created.

Using sandpaper to shape the pencil point

Demonstration 2
Sketching: Holding Your Pencil, Pen or Brush

Fig 1. Fingers

When first holding a pencil for drawing most people adopt the writing position (Fig 1). They rest their hand on the paper and hold the pencil in their fingers. This gives a small controlled area and allows for sketching lines and curves of a short length. This is fine for writing but is not practical for sketching and painting.

By lifting the hand off the page you can work from your wrist as well as your fingers (Fig 2). A single line or curve drawn from the wrist can be two to three times longer than a line drawn from the fingers when the hand is resting on the table.

Sit back in your chair with your hand still off the page. Try drawing a line from your elbow joint (Fig 3). This will give you more freedom to draw longer, free flowing lines. You will have a much larger area for your hand and arm to sweep curved and straight lines.

Finally, with your sketch pad on an easel or a table top, stand up and draw a line using your entire arm and shoulder (Fig 4). This will give you the largest possible area for your arm and hand to sweep and work within.

Try sketching lines on your sketch pad in the ways described above , working from your fingers, wrist, elbow and shoulder.

Fig 2. Wrist

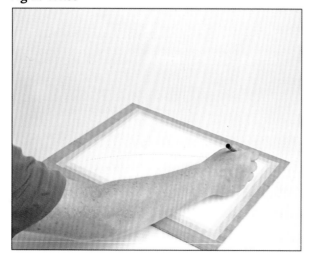

Fig 3. Elbow

Fig 4. Shoulder

Demonstration 3
Basic Shapes

By taking things step by step and building on sound foundations you will soon find that you can begin to sketch successfully. Rather than sketching your subject from the top and working downwards, I recommend a slightly different approach. Everything you ever draw or paint will be based on one or more basic shapes; circles, ovals, squares, rectangles, triangles and cylinders. For an apple, lightly draw a simple circle. The distinctive apple shape can be sketched over that. For a coffee mug, draw a light vertical cylinder and sketch your mug on that. A combination of basic shapes makes the sketching of a traditional telephone quite an easy task. Draw a simple triangle, add a circle for a dial, two ovals and a curve for the handset and a long rectangle for the base.

Lightly drawing the basic shape, or shapes, of your subject will ensure it is going to sit in the right place on your sketch pad, and be of the right proportions. The subject should sit neither too high nor too low on the page, nor be too wide, too thin, too tall nor too short.

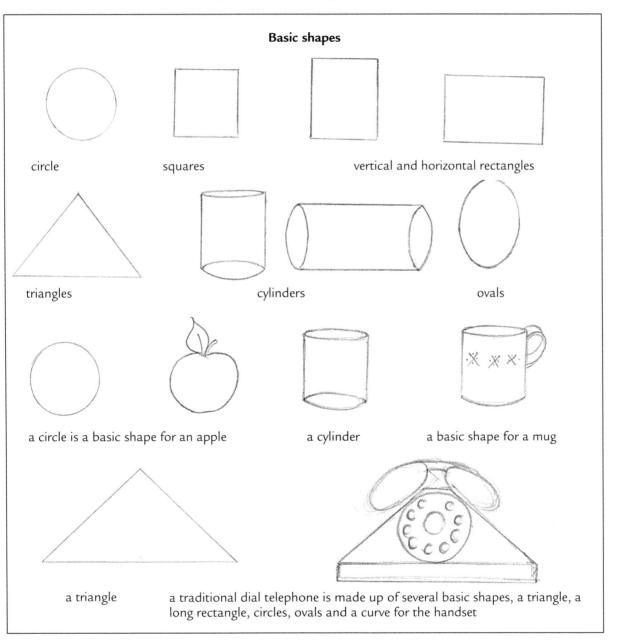

Basic shapes

circle squares vertical and horizontal rectangles

triangles cylinders ovals

a circle is a basic shape for an apple a cylinder a basic shape for a mug

a triangle a traditional dial telephone is made up of several basic shapes, a triangle, a long rectangle, circles, ovals and a curve for the handset

Look around your home for objects based on basic shapes.
Circles, squares, rectangles, cylinders, ovals and triangles.
Sketch the basic shapes and then build the objects on them.

cylinder

saucepan

circle

teapot

triangle

table lamp

square

kitchen scale

Demonstration 4
Pencil Shading

Pencils vary in degree of softness (B) and hardness (H). Copy the chart on the right into your sketch book. H pencils to the left and B pencils to the right. Your kit comes with 7 pencils, each of which has a different number and letter on the end. Find your 2B pencil, and go to No. 2 under letter B and shade a dark to light column down the page. Vary the strength of shading by varying the pressure of your hand on the pencil. As you complete the chart using your remaining pencils you will see and feel the difference in their effects.

Next take your 2B pencil to make the tone chart shown below, left. This will help you get a feeling for the pressure you need to apply in order to achieve different tones; or degrees of "lightness" and "darkness" with your pencil. Experiment with the other pencils to see if you can create the same effects. Soft pencil shading can be gently blended by rubbing with your fingertip for softer shading effects.

In the bottom right panel I show how highlights can be "lifted out" with a kneaded eraser avoiding ragged-edged highlights.

Pencil strength chart

Pencil tonal strengths and blending technique

Lifting out highlights with a kneaded eraser

17

Demonstration 5
Shading: Points To Remember

The sketches on this page are worth copying into your sketch book as they will help you remember the important aspects of shading.

Jug (right). Decide which way the source of light is coming from; the left, the right or from above the subject. This will determine which way the shadow will fall (see diagram below). Here it is from the left, so the shadow is on the right of the jug. I show light shading, then medium and then dark on the right side of the jug. I then emphasized the very darkest features and picked out the highlights.

Below right. The ball and box show the two parts of shadow: the shadow on the object itself, as well as the shadow it casts onto the ground. Note the box casts two shadows, one inside and one outside. The shadow is darkest at the base of the object and becomes lighter as it travels away.

Below left. Refer to the diagram below to see how the placement of the light source in your sketch affects the shadow case by the subject.

Jug

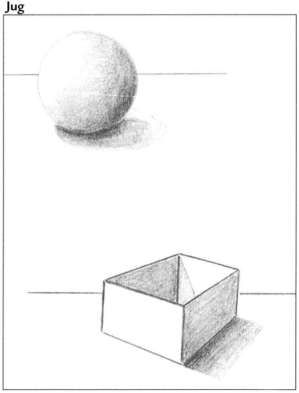

The **higher** the source of light the shorter the shadow

Always decide where the light source is coming from to light your subject, above, the left, the right, behind or in front.

Light from **above**

Light from the **right,**

Light from the **left.**

Light from the **left,** but a low sun →

The **lower** the source of light, the longer the shadows.

The **stronger** the light, the darker the shadow.
The **softer** the light, the gentler the shadow

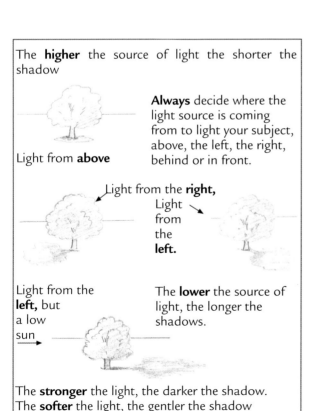

Length of shadow

The shadows objects cast

Demonstration 6
Hatching and Crosshatching

So far we have looked at what I call traditional pencil shading where you achieve varying tones by altering the pressure on your pencil. There is another technique in which you can use a variety of pencil lines to create many other shading effects. They come under four headings.

HATCHING is the use of parallel lines. The closer together the pencil lines, the darker the area; the further apart, the lighter the area.

CROSSHATCHING is where one set of hatching lines is placed over another set.

STIPPLING is where dots are made with the pencil. The closer the dots are, the darker the area; the further apart, the lighter the area.

RANDOM LINES are pencil marks, semicircles, ticks and wiggly pencil effects that do not fall under the other three headings, but can be very useful. Draw the chart below in your sketch book. Invent several more types of hatching, crosshatching and random lines of your own. The tree to the right shows how versatile this technique can be.

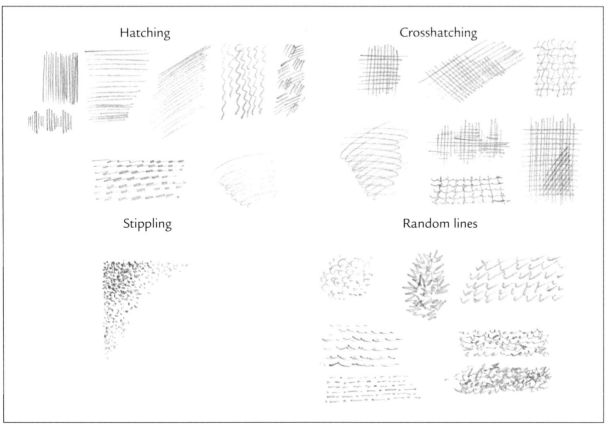

Hatching

Crosshatching

Stippling

Random lines

Demonstration 7
Textures: Tactile Values

A painting consists of three main parts: the sketch or drawing of the subject, the coloring in of it and the ability to show, or suggest, the material the subject is made from.

When you look at paintings by the great masters such as Rembrandt, Gainsborough or Renoir, you do not have to guess what the material was they were painting in any part of their picture. As artists, what we are trying to do is to trick the eyes of the onlooker into believing that a few marks of a pencil on paper is nothing of the sort, but is wood, silk, metal, hair, flesh, or what ever it is we are sketching. In fact, if you think of yourself as an illusionist you will be very close to understanding what much of sketching and painting is about.

We can use the traditional shading, hatching, crosshatching, stippling and random lines to gain an insight into the art of rendering textures, often referred to as tactile values. I would like you to find and sketch two very different pieces of wood, one a piece of rough tree bark, the other a smoother piece. I show these types of wood below. With one I have used hatching and crosshatching to help convey the coarse, rough surface, and with the other I have used a softer, blended shading for the smoother effect. When you have tried this exercise, look around your home for a selection of subjects with a variety of different textures. A rubber glove, a broken brick, a milk bottle or glass and a child's furry toy are excellent examples. See if you can capture the textural effects of the subjects. When you show the resulting sketches to your friends or family, ask them what types of material they think the items are made from. If you are given the correct answer, well done. If they give a wrong answer, look at the surface of the object again and see if there is any more textural information you can add to your sketch. It is well worth trying two or three sketches each month of different textured items in order to continue to develop your skill in capturing textural effects.

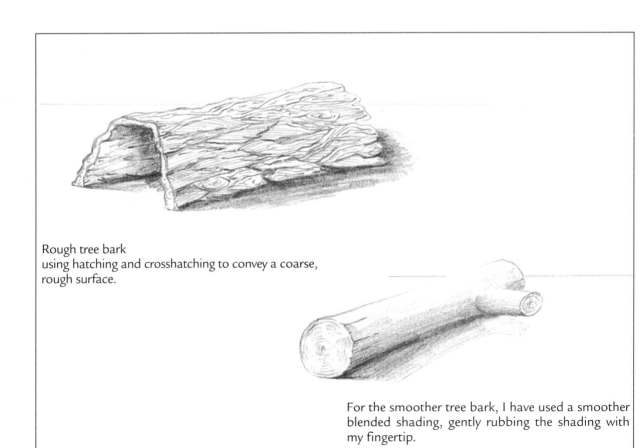

Rough tree bark
using hatching and crosshatching to convey a coarse, rough surface.

For the smoother tree bark, I have used a smoother blended shading, gently rubbing the shading with my fingertip.

Demonstration 8
Planning Your Picture: Still Life

Failing to plan is planning to fail. This is sound advice which applies to almost everything in life, and certainly to sketching and painting. Always choose subjects that you feel moved or inspired by. Never just paint a subject for the sake of it. It is always more enjoyable to paint inspirational subjects and this is often reflected in the quality of the work. Once you have chosen a subject, a little thought and planning goes a long way in helping ensure that you finish with a successful painting. Sketching plays a very important part in the picture planning stage. In the later stages of this book we look at picture composition, but I consider the making of preliminary sketches so important that I think this aspect should be considered at this stage. I will now take a still life subject and a lansdcape to illustrate the uses and advantages of making preliminary sketches.

Preliminary Sketch 1

I set up a simple still life subject on a table. I used a mixing bowl, two eggs, a wooden spoon, a jug and a bag of flour. I wanted to be sure of the correct positions and proportions of the items in the still life in relation to the picture area on my sketch pad. Preliminary Sketch 1 gave me this opportunity.

Preliminary Sketch 2

Here I looked for and added more detail to the shape of the objects to give them a more definite form.

Preliminary Sketch 3

In the third, far more completed sketch on the page opposite, I decided on the direction and strength of the light, I located the light, medium and dark tones, I identified the darkest features and highlights, and finally I positioned the shadows. These three quite quick sketches helped me to really get to know the subject and to identify and resolve any problem areas. At this stage I knew if I were to go ahead and use these preliminary sketches as the basis for a painting I would have sound foundation.

HANDY HINT
Make the first two preliminary sketches the same size as your finished painting. Ideally the finished preliminary sketch should also be the same size, but if it is going to be a large painting then the finished preliminary sketch can be 9"x12" or 12" x 18".

Preliminary Sketch 1

Preliminary Sketch 2

Preliminary Sketch 3

Demonstration 9
Let's Paint a Landscape

With the landscape subject I used exactly the same sequence of steps as before, working from a simple preliminary sketch, below, to a more defined, light, outline sketch, top right on the page opposite, through to the shaded in, more defined sketch, below it. This approach may sound elementary to readers who are at an advanced stage in their painting, but it is a method I have used for over thirty years and it has never let me down. It is an excellent technique for people who are at the start of their sketching and painting activities and well worth more experienced painters trying out. Often the most successful of my students and course members are those who have adopted this approach. They find their paintings are based on a more sound foundation than those who do not use it.

People often choose the first view of a subject they see, only to find that when they stop, stand up, and move from one side to another they find a more interesting or unusual view that they wish they had worked from. If working from life, especially outdoors, it is well worth making several very quick sketches of your subject from different angles to discover the best angle for the subject, even though you may end up coming back to work from the first view or angle you saw.

HANDY HINT

Most of the mistakes in a painting are made before the paintbrush is picked up. People are so keen to get on with the painting they quickly sketch out the picture, spend many hours painting on that sketch, only to find at the end any mistakes in the sketch have been painted into the picture.

When you have made your sketch, BEFORE you shade it or paint it, STOP, turn the sketch upside down, or turn it to face a mirror and look at it in the mirror. Any mistake will show up and can be corrected. The corrections can be rechecked using the same methods

---

Preliminary Sketch 1

Preliminary Sketch 2

Preliminary Sketch 3

Demonstration 10
Pen and Ink Sketching

We have looked at the use of a pencil for sketching, but there are many other items and materials which can be used by artists to create an extensive range of sketching techniques and to allow for the widest varieties of style and expression. Let us look at the use of pen and ink.

Pen and ink sketching is traditionally created using a bottle of black waterproof India ink and a dip-in pen. Most art shops and stationery stores keep mapping pens, or pen holders with separate pen nibs. While nylon and felt-tip pens, technical drawing pens, and fountain pens can be used, so can sharpened matchsticks, toothpicks and sharpened bamboo.

PEN AND INK TECHNIQUE
Keep a spare piece of paper on the table by your side, so that as you dip into the bottle of ink you can test the pen stroke on the paper. This will ensure that there is not too much ink on the nib and that it won't blot. You may get one or two blots at first, but you soon get to know just how much ink to have on your pen. Keep a tissue in your non-painting hand so that every five minutes or so you can wipe your nib on it to stop the ink drying and clogging. The types of drawing lines you will make with pen and ink are similar to those I demonstrated earlier as pencil shading techniques.

HATCHING is where parallel lines are used side by side in any, direction. The closer the lines are together, the darker the area; the further apart they are, the lighter the area.

CROSSHATCHING is where the hatching lines are crossed over each other to achieve an effect.

STIPPLING is simply dots created with the tip of the pen. The more dots on an area, the darker it will become; the fewer dots, the lighter it will be.

RANDOM LINES are any type of line not covered in the other three groups. They could be tick-like marks suggesting tiles on a roof, or semicircles which could be used to create bushes and trees. On a piece of sketching paper practise the hatching, crosshatching, stippling and random lines I show in the panel on the right. When you have tried these, experiment and see how many other types of pen mark and effects you can achieve. Also practise varying the pressure you apply to the nib, the heavier the pressure, the thicker the line; the gentler the pressure, the finer the line.

The pictures on currency notes often incorporate extensive use of hatching, crosshatching and random lines shown in the right hand panel.Experiment by drawing everyday items in pen and ink around your

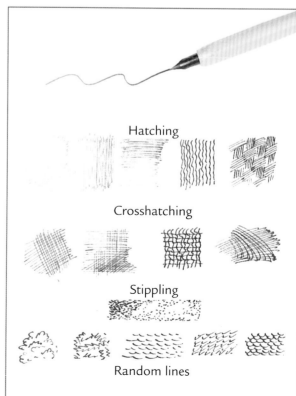

Hatching

Crosshatching

Stippling

Random lines

home and garden. Draw the outline of the items lightly first with a pencil, then overdraw with pen and ink. Leave some items as a pen outline; the simplicity of this approach can be effective. Then try sketching similar items using hatching and crosshatching to create the textures and shading. Use a kneaded eraser when the pen and ink sketch is dry to lift out any pencil guidelines. With practice you will soon discover just the right amount of hatching and crosshatching to use. Look for other examples of pen and ink sketches you may find around your home, school or local library.

HANDY HINT Stand your bottle of India ink in a clean plastic container such as a margarine tub. This way, if you happen to catch it with your pen or tip it over, the spills will be contained and easily cleaned.

A salt mill

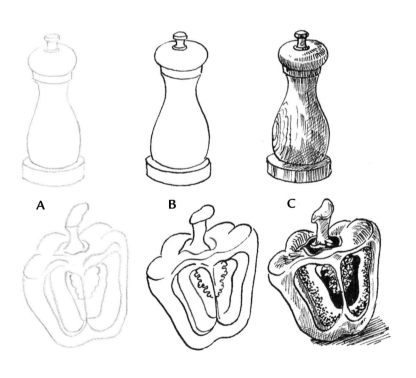

A

B

C

A red pepper cut in half

Look around the house and kitchen to find everyday objects to draw in pen and ink.

A. Sketch the object out in pencil.

B. Draw the outline in India ink with your pen.

C. Using hatching, crosshatching, stippling and random lines, add the shading and textural effects.

Demonstration 11
Roadside Houses

I sketched this view in the delightful village of Churchtown on the outskirts of Southport.

Stage 1. Sketch the subject in light outline using a 2B pencil on sketching paper.

Stage 2. Lightly draw in the outline with pen and ink.

Stage 1

Stage 2

Stage 3. The light source is coming from the left, so the shadows are on the right of the objects in the sketch. The contrast between light and dark plays an important part in the success of the picture. Start using hatching and crosshatching to build up the shadows in each area. Use random lines to give the roof-tiles look, brickwork, foliage of the trees, texture of the foreground tree trunk, grass texture and windows in the way I show in the detail panel, below. If you try the pen and ink sketches in demonstrations 10 and 11, you should have an excellent start to understanding pen and ink sketching. Now go looking for more subjects of your own on which to practise this technique.

Stage 3

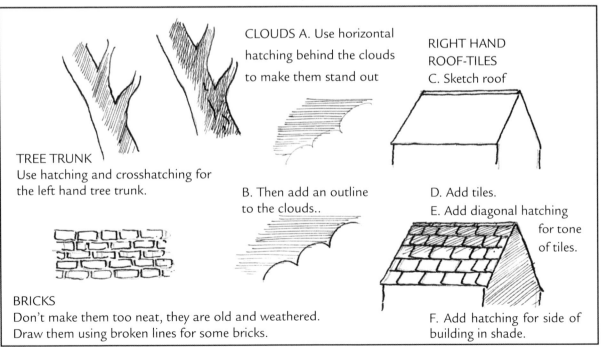

CLOUDS A. Use horizontal hatching behind the clouds to make them stand out

RIGHT HAND ROOF-TILES
C. Sketch roof

TREE TRUNK
Use hatching and crosshatching for the left hand tree trunk.

B. Then add an outline to the clouds..

D. Add tiles.
E. Add diagonal hatching for tone of tiles.

BRICKS
Don't make them too neat, they are old and weathered. Draw them using broken lines for some bricks.

F. Add hatching for side of building in shade.

Detail

Demonstration 12
Stippling: Candle

In the panel on page 26 showing types of pen marks I illustrated an area with stippling. Stippling is done using the tip of the pen to create dots. This can be a fascinating way of creating pictures. In this demonstration I show a candle in a candle stick holder. Try this out, and then see if you can find other subjects that would suit this technique.

Stage 1. Sketch the subject out lightly with your 2B pencil.

Stage 2. Using either your dip-in pen, or a medium or fine felt or nylon-tip pen, start from the top of the candle working your way down the picture stippling the whole subject. Use less dots in the lighter areas, increase them in the medium toned areas and add even more as each area, or part, becomes darker. Try to keep all the dots a similar size. Finally add the shadows of the background drape and tablecloth. Pastels, colored pencils, colored felt-tip pens, oil paint and acrylic paint can also be used for creating stippling paintings. The stippling technique was made very popular by the French artist, Georges Seurat.

Stage 1

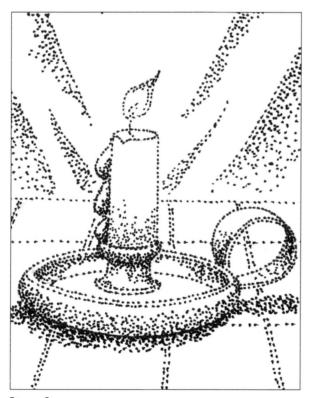

Stage 2

Close up of stippling dots

Demonstration 13
Monochrome with Pen and Ink

The demonstration of the duck in the diagram to the side is an excellent way of recognizing and understanding the value of monochrome studies.

Stage 1. Make a tone strip like the one below by mixing small amounts of India ink with water on your pallet, adding more water to create the lighter tones and less for the darker tones.

Stage 2. Draw the outline of the duck using a 2B pencil

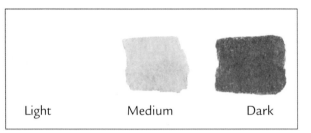

| Light | Medium | Dark |

Tonal Test Strip

Stage 3. Brush the lightest tone on the duck as shown. Leave white paper for highlights, and let it dry.

Stage 4. Apply your medium tone as shown and let dry.

Stage 5. Apply your darkest tone last as shown and let dry.

Stage 6. Overdraw your pencil lines with pen and ink.

This demonstration helps you to understand about tone and the role it plays in sketching and painting. When you have tried the demonstration, look for subjects in color and try sketching them using this monochrome technique.

I often make monochrome studies, either for my own enjoyment, or as advanced preliminary sketches for major paintings. I have selected three monochrome sketches painted over the recent years from my portfolio. These are shown on the next page.

Monochrome Studies From My Portfolio

Top right. I saw my mother's steam iron on the kitchen table and found the monochrome technique helped me resolve the tricky problems in sketching this subject. I took an oblique view from above, looking down onto the iron. I used diluted India ink and then a felt-tipped pen to overdraw the pencil lines.

Bottom left. The Customs House, Kings Lynn. I made this monochrome sketch on location, and used it as a preliminary sketch towards making a finished painting of the subject. I used India ink and a dip-in pen to overdraw the pencil lines.

Bottom right. There are subjects all around us. I once simply opened the bathroom door, sat on the landing floor, which gave me a lower eyelevel, and sketched our bathroom sink in monochrome using diluted writing ink, and then overdrew it with a felt-tipped pen.

Iron

Customs House, Kings Lynn

Bathroom Sink

Demonstration 14
Pen and Wash with Water Colors - Cottage By The Sea

The previous demonstrations and advice provide a good foundation for all your future art work. Let me now introduce you to the joys of sketching with pen and wash in color. A pocket set of water colors, a No. 6 or No. 8 round water color brush, two glasses of water, a water color sketch pad, a 2B pencil, a kneaded eraser, together with your pen and ink, are all you need for this versatile technique.

Stage 1. Sketch out the subject with a 2B pencil.

Stage 2. Mix and apply a pale wash of color for each area. Let it dry.

Stage 3. Mix and apply a medium tone wash for each area, leaving parts of the lighter tones showing through.

Stage 4. Mix a darker wash and apply it as shown in the Stage 3 picture. When dry, use a dip-in pen or a felt-tip pen and oversketch the picture. The resulting picture should have a sharp, crisp look to it. This technique can be used for producing quick sketches and finished art work.

Stage 1

Stage 2

Stage 3

Stage 4

Santorini

SANTORINI · GREECE.

Philip Berill 1987.

Notre Dame de Paris

A water color or oil painting may take several hours to paint, but a pen and wash sketch can be completed in a fraction of the time. It is for this reason I often use this technique outdoors.

When I am out with family or friends, or travelling, I often see splendid and appealing subjects, but due to the very limited time available it is not possible to paint a finished picture. Pen and wash with water color enables me to make a quick sketch, splash color onto it, and overdraw the essentials with my pen and ink. I then not only have a presentable and attractive sketch in its own right, but a sketch that provides material which can be developed into a finished painting in my studio. Let me show you several situations where I used the technique quickly to produce pictures which have a freshness or added quality that may have been lost by having unlimited time available to paint them.

Santorini. Left.

I was tutoring on a cruise, sailing from Venice to Corfu, Dubrovnik, Santorini, through the Corinth Canal to Athens and on to Turkey. My task was to teach and demonstrate to the students on the cruise, not to go off painting my own pictures. But in free moments, coffee breaks and lunch breaks I would take out my pen and wash kit and sketch a view which caught my eye, like the breathtaking view in Santorini on the page opposite. The composition with the domed roof breaking the line of its distant hills was exciting and I only had fifteen minutes to capture the scene. I used water colors on sketching paper, overdrawing it with a fine felt-tip pen. Santorini, just for the price of a cup of coffee.

Notre Dame de Paris. Below.

Most people like to paint Notre Dame from the front. I was walking along the Left Bank in Paris, turned around and saw this rear view of Notre Dame. I knew I had to paint this view but it was soon going to rain. As a water color would have taken too long, I chose to do a pen and wash. The sketch took thirty minutes and I was packing away my materials as the first rain drops started to fall.

Venice

Gondolas are as much a part of Venice as are the pigeons in St. Mark's Square. The joy of the city is that it has not had to be adapted to accommodate automobiles. Venice is a marriage of sea and land. Venice is liquid light, a place where the sounds and sights which have captivated artists, musicians and authors over the past centuries have also cast its magic spell over me.

Below. Become an explorer. On one visit to Venice I decided to visit an area of the city unknown to me. I fortunately had my pen and wash kit with me when I came across the last gondola boatyard in Venice. The sketch below took forty-five minutes using a felt-tip pen over a water color sketch painted on 140 lb paper.

I was intrigued by the single large tree in the center of the boatyard. This apparently has a design purpose; it is there to provide shade during the heat of the day for the boatyard workers. I was also intrigued to see the gondolas on their sides for repair... not quite the graceful upright position we see as they glide along the canals of the city.

Right. On another occasion I was teaching on one of my painting holiday courses in Venice. A particular view across the Grand Canal had often caught my eye and I felt it had the makings of a good subject. I liked the long, slender buildings and the Venetian lamppost. I discovered that if I sat on the pavement it would give me a low eyelevel and would have the effect of the lamppost appearing to intersect the line of the roofs. The top of the lamppost would be seen set against the sky. The lamppost also acted to link the foreground, the Grand Canal and the buildings on the other side of the canal. For speed I used pen and wash with water color to capture one of my favorite views on paper.

HANDY HINT. Pen and wash is addictive. Do not get hooked on it. The technique enables charming pictures to be produced so quickly that there is a temptation to draw black pen lines around every water color painting to finish the picture quickly. Don't let pen and wash studies be more than 25% of your picture production. This way you will retain the enjoyment of the technique to the overall benefit of your painting.

Gondola Boatyard, Venice.

View across the Grand Canal, Venice

Demonstration 15
Flowers. Daffodil

How fortunate we are to be surrounded by so much natural beauty. Throughout the seasons we have an ever-changing wealth of flowers in our gardens, parks and floral shops. We grow them for our enjoyment and send cut flowers and potted plants as gifts to relatives and friends on special occasions. While floral painting deserves a whole book to itself, you can start to sketch flowers from the very first day you pick up a pencil and paper. I have shown several sketches which you may like to try. They are an excellent way to start floral subjects.

Daffodil.

This was a single bloom with leaves from our garden, cut and placed in a tall, thin, clear, glass vase of water. The vase had a heavy base. I allowed the flower to curve slightly to the right, rather than have everything too straight. Choose a similar subject from your garden or use this study. Sketch the subject out with a 2B pencil. Using water colors tint the flower, stem and leaves of the flower, leaving the vase in pencil. The idea of using just a splash of color in a sketch, to focus attention on the main feature, can give a distinctive look.

Rose.

At first, choose flowers with distinctive petals and leaves, do not paint very small flowers. The rose is perhaps one of the most beautiful of flowers. I bought this single rose for my daughter but could not resist sketching it. From one rose you can produce four different types of sketch and learn so much about each technique and the structure of the flower. The top left study shows the rose just in pencil outline. The top right study is a pencil sketch with the addition of shading. The bottom left study is a water color sketch. Finally try the sketch in water color overdrawn with pen and ink. One subject, four different treatments. If you try four studies of a different flower each month, you will soon gain expertise in sketching and painting flowers.

Demonstration 16
Rose

Pencil outline

Pencil with shading

Water color

Water color overdrawn with pen and ink

Demonstration 17
Color Notes

As we are now using water colors as an important part of adding color to our sketches, you will find it helpful to make out the color chart on the right. While most water color boxes have a good selection of colors in them, many colors can be made by mixing just three PRIMARY COLORS, Red, Yellow and Blue. By mixing any two of the three primary colors, you make the SECONDARY COLORS. Red and Yellow make Orange, Yellow and Blue make Green, Blue and Red make Mauve. If you mix any two of the secondary colors, you make the TERTIARY COLORS. Orange and Mauve make Dark Brown, Orange and Green make Light Brown, and Mauve and Green make Olive Green. By mixing the three PRIMARY COLORS, Red, Yellow and Blue, with very little water you can make Black. Brown and Blue mixed together will make Grey.

The water color sketch shown below is of items that were lying on our kitchen table one morning, an eggcup, a spoon and a knife. This sketch was painted using colors made by mixing the three primary colors.

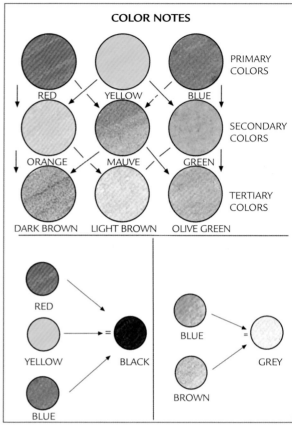

COLOR NOTES

RED   YELLOW   BLUE — PRIMARY COLORS

ORANGE   MAUVE   GREEN — SECONDARY COLORS

DARK BROWN   LIGHT BROWN   OLIVE GREEN — TERTIARY COLORS

RED
YELLOW
BLUE
= BLACK

BLUE
BROWN
= GREY

Demonstration 18
Pinocchio: Mixed Media

It is important to learn how different mediums can impart their own distinct look to a subject. In this demonstration I used Pinocchio, a wooden doll I once bought for my daughter. He is a cheerful fellow and very colorful.

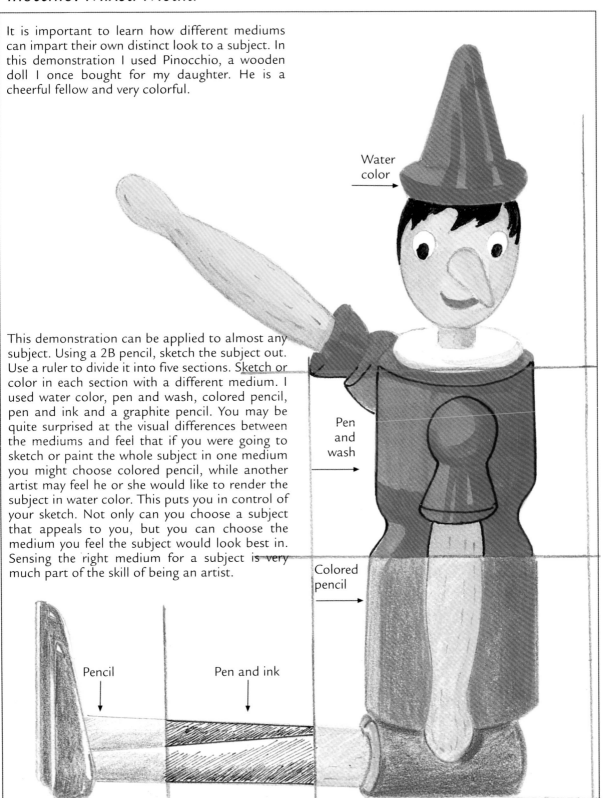

Water color

Pen and wash

Colored pencil

Pencil

Pen and ink

This demonstration can be applied to almost any subject. Using a 2B pencil, sketch the subject out. Use a ruler to divide it into five sections. Sketch or color in each section with a different medium. I used water color, pen and wash, colored pencil, pen and ink and a graphite pencil. You may be quite surprised at the visual differences between the mediums and feel that if you were going to sketch or paint the whole subject in one medium you might choose colored pencil, while another artist may feel he or she would like to render the subject in water color. This puts you in control of your sketch. Not only can you choose a subject that appeals to you, but you can choose the medium you feel the subject would look best in. Sensing the right medium for a subject is very much part of the skill of being an artist.

Composition

The techniques we have looked at thus far, the use of color, light and shade and the illusion of textural effects are all important aspects in your sketches. Equally important is the composition of your sketch. There are certain guidelines that, if followed, can help to build a sound compositional foundation for your work.

The Half-way Rule

One important rule is to not have any line or object cut your picture into two equal halves in order to avoid monotony in the composition. Note how in Views A and B below, the views are cut in half horizontally by the horizon and vertically by the tree trunk. By setting the horizon slightly lower (View C) and offsetting the tree trunk to the left of center (View D) the composition becomes much more dynamic and visually interesting.

Focal Points and Key Lines

When looking at your work, the viewer's eyes should not be wandering around the sketch as though lost. You are the artist; you are in control, so decide what it is that you want people to be looking at in particular. In other words, your picture should have a FOCAL POINT, or a main feature to which the eyes are led.

In View E, the focal point is the barn, set in the distance. In View F, it is the castle in the far distance, and in View G it is the shed in the foreground.

I have arrowed the KEY LINES in each view as well so that you can see how the details in the pictures follow these key lines and lead the viewers eye to the focal points helping to bring the entire composition together.

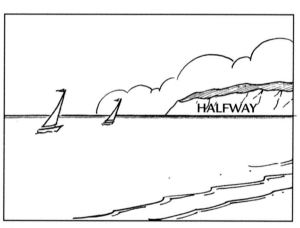

View A

View C

View B

View D

View E

View F

THE TRIANGLE

A triangular shape often makes for a good picture composition. If you look at many of the paintings or prints that catch your eye and analyse them, they will have an underlying triangular structure to the composition.

I show three triangular compositions. In H, the still life, the table lamp and spectacles form the upright side of the triangle. In I, the tree to the right of the bridge helps form the apex of the triangle, which is just to the right of the center of the picture. In J, the apex is on the right of the picture, and the sloping top edge of the triangle takes us to the building which is the focal point of the picture.

A good composition should have a sense of height, width and depth. The triangular shape is often helpful in ensuring this is achieved.

View G

View H

View I

View J

Perspective

Perspective is the one area of drawing and painting in which most people experience some degree of difficulty. When people hear perspective mentioned, they often go to a bookshop or a library, obtain a book on the subject, flip through it, see lines shooting about all over the place and usually end up more confused than before they opened the book. The secret is to keep the whole business of perspective as simple as possible, to remember a few basic rules, and to bear in mind that perspective is not something one masters in one, two or three lessons. Learning about perspective is an ongoing process. One goes along over a period of months, indeed years, collecting together the pieces of information, like pieces of a jigsaw, until they all fit together and the picture, the theory of perspective becomes clear and easy to apply to one's work.

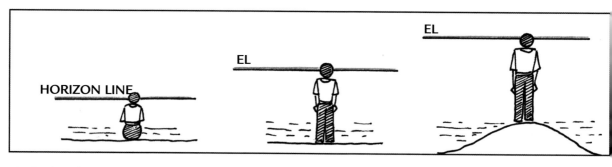

The horizon line is an imaginary line across your field of vision when you look straight on; not up or down, but straight ahead. In my sketch you see how the horizon line stays directly in front of the subject regardless if he is sitting down, standing level, or standing higher on a dune. To determine the horizon line when looking at a real subject, hold a ruler by its thin side, horizontally in front of your eyes. This is where the horizon line should be in your composition. Generally, I suggest that you draw the subject lightly first, though, then apply your horizon line to your sketch. Your horizon line is then used to help apply perspective to the rest of your work and to check and correct your subject.

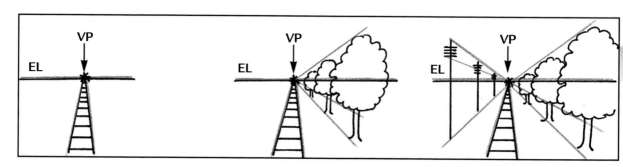

Perspective is a system of creating an illusion of three dimensions in objects in your sketch. One way to see perspective in action is to picture the view looking down railroad tracks. The rail ties appear to become smaller and closer together until the tracks merge and disappear. The point where the tracks appear to merge is the "Vanishing Point" (VP), which you will note is a point on the Horizon Line. We know that they don't merge in reality, however by having them vanish on the horizon line we create the illusion that they are getting further away and that the scene has depth. My sketch illustrates this, and I show the tracks with three trees to the right, and then also with telephone poles to the left. Both the trees and the poles appear to become smaller and close together as well as they recede. I have shown the guide lines for each item, illustrating how the guidelines all meet at the vanishing point on the horizon line.

Next I show a front view of a tool box. With this view here is just one vanishing point on the horizon line for the sides of the box. I am imagining that I am sitting on a chair at a table, drawing the box in front of me. If I look straight ahead, over the box, my horizon line would be about 12" (30.5cm) above the top of the tool box. In my next sketch the box is set at an angle. We now have two vanishing points, one for each side. Guidelines will often want to converge at vanishing points off the page. This is quite normal and often happens. When it does, lay scrap paper at the side and tape it on from behind, then extend the guidelines onto it, in the way I show in my sketch. Never guess or assume the perspective is correct, always try to prove it.

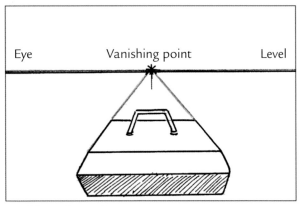

Tool box, front view

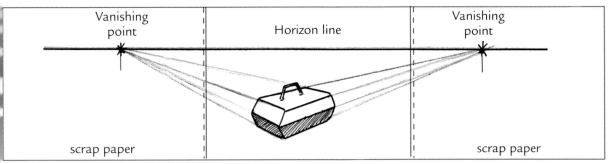

Tool box at an angle

Circular perspective.

A church at an angle with 2 V.P.s

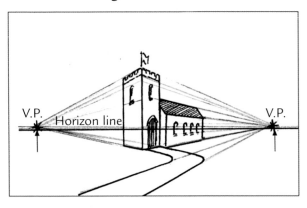

Very few people realise that perspective can be used to help solve the problem of drawing circular and elliptical subjects, but it can. I have illustrated this with my sketch of two paint cans and a paint roller. I have drawn the subject out and placed my horizon line well above it. I have then drawn a light guiding square around each ellipse and have drawn those squares "in perspective", in the same way as the tool box. The squares for the ellipses each have their perspective vanishing points on the common horizon line. Both the large can and the small can share the same vanishing point as those ellipses are on the same plane. The ellipses for the paint roller are set at an angle, on a different plane, and have a vanishing point on the horizon line, but over to the left. Using the squares helps determine where each vanishing point should be, to ensure the true perspective of the subject when an ellipse is involved. I then go back to each square to check that the ellipse touches the center of each side of the square it occupies, for provided it does, I know the ellipse must be in true perspective. The squares and guidelines can be gently rubbed out before you shade or paint your picture.

Circular perspective. Paint cans and roller

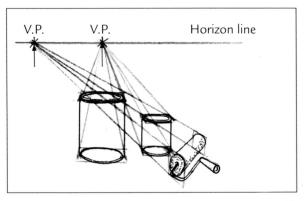

Demonstration 19
Faces

This demonstration is intended as a quick guide. Drawing faces is a subject that deserves an entire book, however, there are a few basic rules that if followed correctly should help you to sketch faces successfully

Sketch A. Rule 1 is that the head is an EGG SHAPE.

Sketch B. The second rule is use HALFWAY LINES. The center of the eyes are on a line halfway between the top of the skull and bottom of the chin. The bottom of the nose is on a line halfway between the center of the eye line and the bottom of the chin. The middle of the mouth is on a line halfway between the bottom of the nose and the chin. The top of the ears are just above the line for the center of the eyes. The bottom of the ears are on the bottom of the nose line.

Sketch C. A vertical line down the center of the face sees the eyes, nose, mouth and ears divided equally either side of it.

Sketch D. I have turned those halfway guidelines into ellipses and placed the features on them. This starts to bring the face into circular perspective and helps with any foreshortening of the face. We can now use head D and start to maneuver it to overcome all sorts of positional problems. Simply turn the egg and guidelines to the left, E, and to the right, F. Point the center of the egg to the left or right and tilt it back, G. We can alter the incline of the head. To give the head backward look, H, place the curves steeper on the egg, or to give the downward look dip the curves downward as in sketch I. This helps achieve the foreshortening of the features and head. The contours of the face, hair and features can be built up on the foundation of the egg shape and guidelines of any face, J. Copy these sketches and then practise using photographs of faces and real faces.

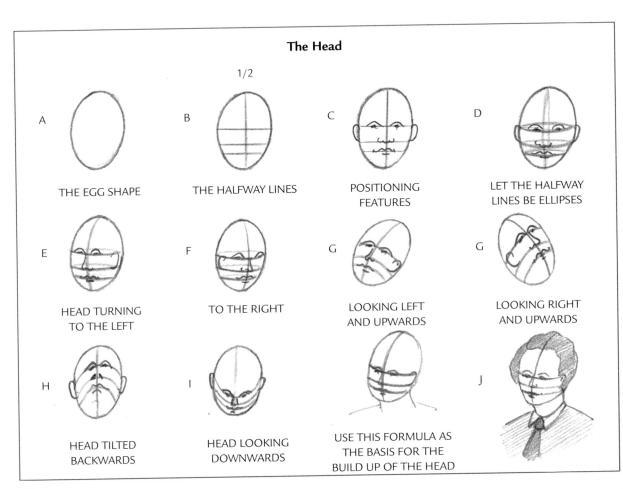

The Head

A — THE EGG SHAPE

B — THE HALFWAY LINES — 1/2

C — POSITIONING FEATURES

D — LET THE HALFWAY LINES BE ELLIPSES

E — HEAD TURNING TO THE LEFT

F — TO THE RIGHT

G — LOOKING LEFT AND UPWARDS

G — LOOKING RIGHT AND UPWARDS

H — HEAD TILTED BACKWARDS

I — HEAD LOOKING DOWNWARDS

USE THIS FORMULA AS THE BASIS FOR THE BUILD UP OF THE HEAD

J

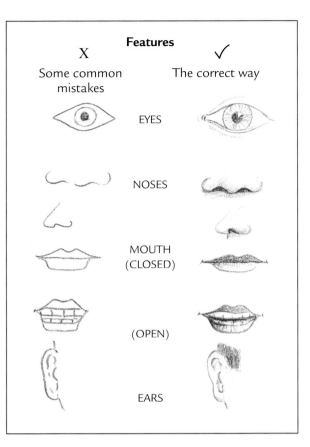

Features

X		✓
Some common mistakes		The correct way

EYES

NOSES

MOUTH (CLOSED)

(OPEN)

EARS

Practise sketching features from photographs and from life. Look in a mirror and sketch your own features. Look at an eye and pay close attention to detail. Note the tear duct in the corner near the nose, the highlight on the black pupil of the eye, the tone of the iris, the way the eyelids clip the top and bottom of the iris. Note the shading on the white of the eye and the shading in the folds of flesh above and below the eyelids. Note the shading under the lobes of the nose and nostril, and the shadow on the top lip.

When the mouth is closed the top lip is very dark. The lower lip has shading, but also highlights. Show the fine lines curving over the lower lip. When the mouth is open hint at the teeth and make the cavity in the mouth very dark. Avoid severe outlines.

The eyes, nose and mouth are dominant features. The ears are a secondary feature. Understate the ears; do not make them as clearly defined as the other features unless it is unavoidable.

Top left. Features
Bottom left. Girl, pencil sketch.
Bottom right. Man, felt-tip pen sketch.

Demonstration 20
Figures

Learning the proportions and developing a practical technique are the keys to sketching figures successfully. There are 8 heads in the length of the male figure, 7½ heads in the length of the female figure and 4½ heads in the young child figure. Copy the proportion sketch on the right to imprint these proportions on your mind.

There are three types of figure in a sketch or painting, the far distant figure, the middle distance figure and the foreground figure. Let us look at proportions and techniques for sketching the middle distance figure as this is the type most often seen in general landscape sketches and paintings. The technique can be applied to all other figures.

Below. I show how to use stick figures to position the figure. I add a chest and pelvis, locate the shoulder, elbow, knee joints, hands and feet. I usually sketch these very lightly in pencil and then sketch the actual figure and clothes on that foundation. The same technique can be used for standing, sitting, static or moving figures. Try pencil and pen and ink sketches of these types of figures. Do not put in too much detail. Keep them simple.

The workman on the train, on the page opposite. This character was sitting just a few yards from me on a train one day. Using water colors oversketched with a felt-tip pen, I found the above figure drawing technique worked equally well for this closer figure.

FIGURES

Proportions of man, woman and child in relation to each other

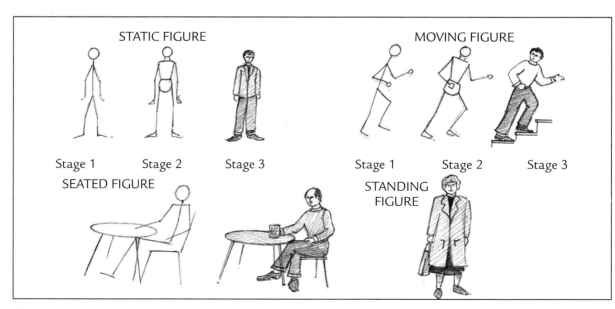

STATIC FIGURE

Stage 1   Stage 2   Stage 3

SEATED FIGURE

MOVING FIGURE

Stage 1   Stage 2   Stage 3

STANDING FIGURE

Workman on Train

Sketch of MANCUNIAN
WORKER ON TRAIN TO
SOUTHPORT. 15·7·70.
P.E.J. BERRILL

Demonstrations 21
Sketching Outdoors

Many people are apprehensive at first about sketching outdoors. There is no need to be. You can simply look out of your window and draw the view you see, or go into your back garden or a friend's garden and sketch a corner of it. There is nothing quite like sketching and painting outdoors. You become very much part of the scene which you are painting. When painting from a photograph everything you see has been frozen for a split second, but compare that to being outdoor, you can feel the warmth of the sun, the gentle breeze, the sky is active, the clouds move, the light changes, any water flows, you can hear the sounds of people, birds or other features which may be part of your subject.

A viewfinder, right, is a window 3" x 2¼" (75mm x 55mm) cut out of a piece of card 9" x 6¼" (230 mm x 160mm). Held at arm's length this can be used to frame various areas of an outdoor view to help you decide what, and how much of the view, you want in your picture. Hold it horizontally, then see if you can find upright views by holding the viewfinder so the rectangle in the center is vertical. Keep the subjects simple and not too cluttered. If you encounter a subject with tricky perspective like the rowing boat shown on the page opposite, use the basic shape idea as discussed on pages 15 and 16. Draw a box, find the center of the top and front. Then draw the boat inside the box with the center line to guide you for the position of the bow and stem.

Peel Harbour, Isle of Man, below. I was intrigued by the long, thin, horizontal picture possibility of this view. I drew a long, thin rectangle on my sketch pad and sketched the subject in pencil and water color.

HANDY HINT.
When sketching outdoors keep the kit light and simple. A sketch pad, 2B pencil, pencil sharpener, putty eraser, pocket set of water colors, a No. 6 or No. 8 round brush, small bottle of water, two small containers to pour the water into, some tissues to clean your brush and a fine felt-tip pen are all you need for many happy hours of outdoor sketching.

Viewfinder

View

Pencil and wash sketch of selected area

Using viewfinder to select subject area

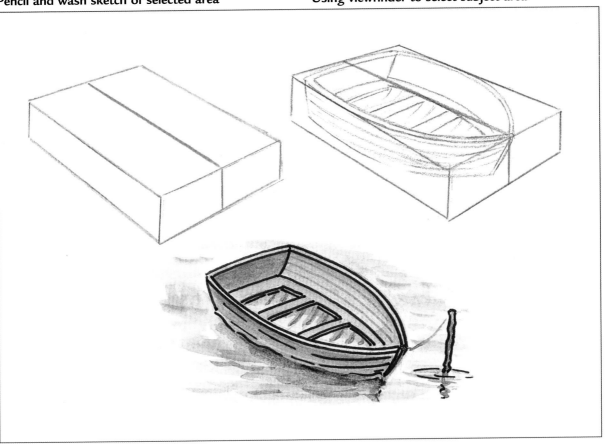

Using a box as the basis for drawing a rowing boat

Demonstration 22
Sketching and Painting from Photographs

Some artist say never copy, only work from life. Others say copying is perfectly acceptable. My feeling is that a camera and photographs can be a great aid to the artist, providing that he or she does not become a slave to them. As a source of back up reference material they have many uses. You can of course learn to paint sunsets, snow, seascapes, animals, foreign views and many other subjects from photographs, perhaps when there is no possibility of doing so from life. A quick outdoor sketch, supported by a photograph you took of the subject, can also provide all the material you need for a future painting at home. Animals, birds and subjects which move too quickly for you to sketch, can be sketched and painted from photographs. The secret is to try to bring the subject to life. This can be achieved with a little imagination, by thinking yourself into the view, or in front of the animal, bird or subject. **A Manx Cottage.** I was on the Isle of Man when I came across this delightful Manx cottage. To obtain the best view meant going into the owners garden, and in such circumstances an artist must ask the owners permission to sketch or to take a photograph. Usually, as on this occasion, the owner is only too pleased to let you take a photograph and make a sketch. As it was late afternoon I did not have the time to paint the cottage. The daylight would soon be lost. The combination of photograph and sketch meant I would be able to work from these to produce a finished painting in my studio.

HANDY HINT. Keep a large envelope or folder by you. Any time you come across a photograph that looks interesting and that could provide reference material for painting, pop it in your envelope

Fountains Abbey. This was a photograph one of my students took. It was a little dark, but had possibilities. I decided that if he made a circular painting, based on the center, it would make an interesting picture. The trees on the left and right were not essential to the painting. This was very much a situation of finding a picture within a picture. I illustrated the idea to him in a sketch.

Stage 1.

The photograph of Fountains Abbey. A good possible subject in the center, too dark at the sides.

Stage 2.

I cut a circle out of a piece of card to frame the area of interest in the photograph.

Stage 3.

I used pen and wash to sketch out the Abbey, the immediate lansdcape and figures. I modified the trees on the left and decided this would provide a good subject for a painting.

Stage 1. Student's photograph

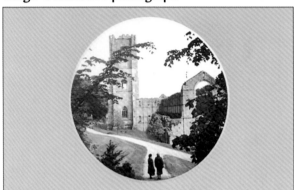

Stage 2. Area of interest

Stage 3. Pen and wash sketch

Sketches for a Mural

Sketches produced on one occasion can sometimes be used on another occasion. I was asked by clients if I would paint a mural for their new, indoor swimming pool. The subject they had in mind was northern Italy and the Italian lakes. I had a folder full of recent sketches of the area, except for the Italian lakes. For the far end wall I combined two sketches, one of Villa Pitiana, a 12th century palace set against the Tuscan hills, the other, a view of a farm at the foot of the Tuscan hills. Although I had not visited the lakes so had no sketches, I decided to use a selection of photographs to compose the subject for the left-hand wall. The whole mural was designed to look as if it were one view.

The two photographs on the right show the finished mural painted in acrylic paint. The sketch immediately below was to show the client how the mural would look in their swimming pool. I also show the original sketch of the Villa Pitiana, right, and the farm, below.

Finished mural. Right-hand wall

Finished mural. Left-hand wall

Sketch of proposed mural for my client

Sketch. Villa Pitiana

Sketch. Tuscan Farm

Demonstration 23
Colored Pencils

Colored pencils provide a convenient way to add color to a sketch. They can be used in a variety of different ways. There are two types of colored pencil, water soluble and non-water soluble. They can be bought in sets or individually. They can be used dry on sketching paper, or wet on a smooth 90lb, or 140lb, water color paper. Try using them dry first. Lightly draw out a subject and then color and shade it with the colored pencils. As with normal graphite pencils you can increase or decrease the tonal strength by varying the pressure you apply. You can also superimpose one color on another to achieve fascinating color variations. I show two sketches using water soluble colored pencils dry. One is of a farm on a hill, the other is a coastal view looking out to sea.

Below. The left half of the farm landscape uses dry colored pencils. On the right half of the farm sketch I have shown how brushing a little water over the colored pencil imparts a water color look to it. When dry, the picture can be oversketched again using the dry technique where appropriate. The view looking out to sea uses dry colored pencils.

Demonstrations 24
Sketching with Pastels

Pastels have been popular for several centuries. Pastels are a mixture of pigment, chalk and pipe clay. They vary from very soft to firm and come in round or square sticks. The artist normally snaps the stick into pieces of different lengths and then sketches and works with the tips, sides and edges of the pastel, applying the dry color directly to the paper. The most common pastel paper is known as Ingres paper. It comes in a range of colors, from light to very dark, and has a slightly coarse texture which enables the pastel to grip the surface.

Pastel sketching is when the artist uses the pastel directly on the paper and lets the color of the paper become an integral part of the picture in the way I have done with my vegetable sketch. One color of pastel can be overlaid on another. Pastel painting is when the finger is used to gently smudge and blend the pastel to achieve often delightful effects. The background paper is fully covered, so the color of the paper is less important.

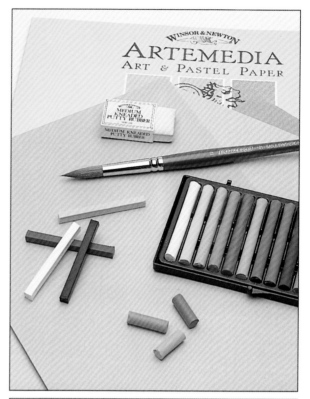

It is also possible to buy pastel pencils. These are encased in wood and the artist works with the point to give a more detailed appearance to the picture. Many artists build up a collection of each type of pastel. Pastel pictures are normally 'fixed' with a light spray of clear fixative to minimise the risk of the pastel smudging accidentally.

A pad, or sheet, of pastel paper, a box of 12 assorted pastels including a white and a black, a can of aerosol fixative, a kneaded eraser and a stiff dry paintbrush are all you need to start pastel sketching. The dry brush is used to jab at any errors to loosen the pastel, which you then gently blow away before rubbing the area with the eraser.

Right. Snap a pastel and try to see how many different marks you can make with it. Vary your hand pressure to increase or decrease the strength of color.

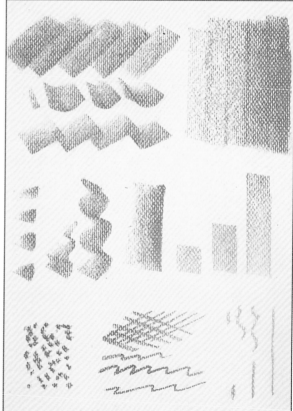

HANDY HINT. Keep a damp cloth in a plastic bag by you so you can take the cloth out to wipe your fingers when working with pastels. This keeps your fingers clean and the bag keeps the cloth damp

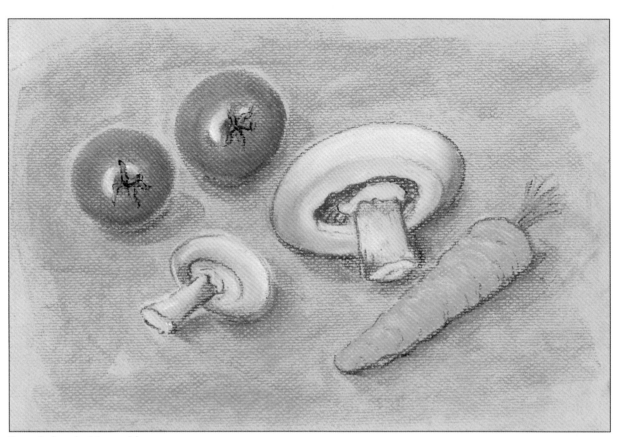

Pastel sketch. Vegetables

Pastel painting. Landscape

Demonstrations 25
Sketching with Oil Paints

Many artists paint with oil paints but do not realise you can use them for sketching. As oil paints normally require several days to become touch dry, many people think they are not a practical medium for sketching. I can tell you of two very successful ways to use them for this purpose.

Tinted Canvas Panel.

If sketching outdoors, take a canvas panel, your oil paints and materials with you, making sure you have some clean turpentine. When you find a subject that appeals to you, sketch it out lightly with a 2B pencil on the canvas panel. Then, mix your oil paints colors with small amounts of turpentine to create a thin consistency. Tint the various colored areas of your canvas with the thinned paint. Within 30 to 60 minutes the turpentine will have evaporated and the panel will be dry. You can then take this panel, and others you may tint, home. On cold, wet, winter days, or dark evenings, take a panel out and paint the fully finished oil painting on top of your original, tinted oil color panel.

The same technique can be used indoors, but lends itself well to outside painting expeditions and holidays.

Liquin.

The other method is to use Liquin, an alkyd resin produced by Winsor and Newton, that you can mix with your oil paints instead of turpentine or linseed oil for normal oil painting techniques. It accelerates the drying of the oil paint. I use it frequently, and find if I am on holiday and mix Liquin with my oil paint to paint the oil paintings at the beginning of the holiday, the pictures are touch dry at the end of the holiday and can, with care, be transported home safely. Alkyd paints are synthetic paints similar to oils, but based in Liquin. They are normally touch dry within 18 hours.

Subject. Lakeland bridge

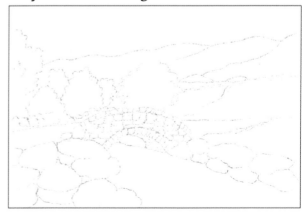

Subject drawn out on a canvas panel

HANDY HINT. Wear old clothes when working with oil paints. Oils are lovely to use, but dabs of color can get on to your clothes, no matter how careful you are.

Partially tinted Oil Panel Sketch

Finished tinted Oil Panel Sketch

Lord Street, Southport

Inspiration and imagination do not come in tubes or bottles. For twelve years I owned an art store and framed pictures. One day a lady asked to have a picture framed. Her husband was a keen fisherman and had been salmon fishing in Scotland. While there he bought a long, thin, pencil sketch of the salmon river with inset sketches of the salmon pools along each side. It was a charming idea and the long, thin shape attracted me. Southport does not have a salmon river, but it has a very famous street over a mile long, called Lord Street. It is very straight and a central feature of the town with many historic buildings, shops and hotels situated either side of it. I thought I could adapt the salmon river idea to the

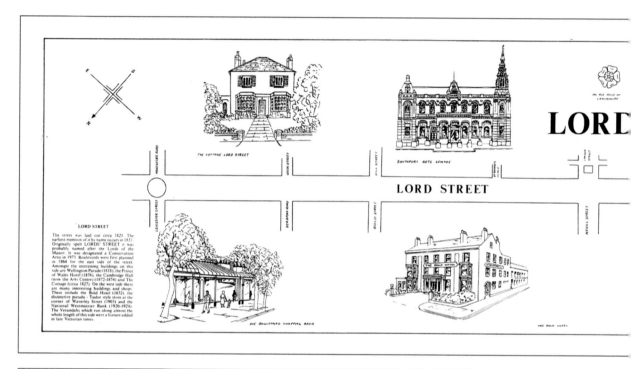

street featuring key buildings and the town's history instead of salmon pools. I selected the most interesting buildings, made sketches of them, and used pen and ink to draw out the finished art work in my studio. I had it screen printed and then sold it framed and unframed, in black and white and hand water colored versions. Measuring 9¼"x 36"(235mm x 910mm) it has proven to be very popular with residents and visitors to the town. Southport's local authority commissioned 200 framed, slightly different versions of the print, to be the town's gift, presented by the Mayors of Southport to very important visitors. Can you adapt a familiar location in an imaginative way?

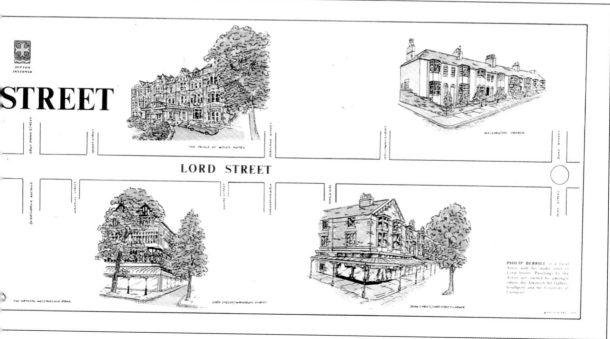

Framing Sketches

Keep loose sketches clean and flat in a portfolio. There will be sketches that you decide to frame and exhibit or sell. Some people make their own frames, but the majority of people call on the help of a professional picture framer, or buy and use many of the very good, ready-made frames and mats which can often be found in art and framing stores. Some framers advertise a mail order service in art catalogues.

Pencil, colored pencils, pen and ink, water color and pastel sketches will need to be framed with a mat of a suitable color and under glass. The glass protects the picture from atmospheric soiling. The mat provides a border between the surrounding wall and the sketch and keeps the glass away from the immediate picture surface.

Oil paint sketches, which are not too thickly painted, can be framed the same way, but generally, and especially if thickly or robustly painted, oil paintings are varnished and framed without glass.

A good framer can be a very good friend, offering expert advice on what will show your sketches and paintings to the best advantage.

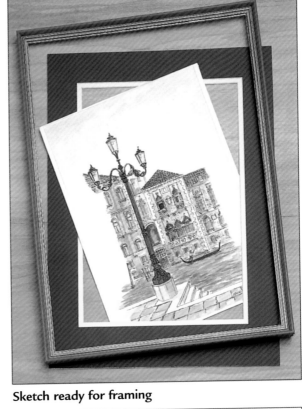

Sketch ready for framing

Picture mats

Framed sketch

Exhibiting and Selling Work

Many people who take up the art of painting never think of the possibility of exhibiting or selling their work. Their first paintings are often given to family and friends, and people begin to see and admire their work. "How much do you want for that painting?" "Do you think you could paint me a picture of such and such?"

How do, you price your pictures? How do you go about selling your work? The price you can command will depend on the type and quality of paintings and the state of the local economy. It would be nice to give a short answer on what to charge, but because of the above conditions I can't... but I can tell you people who can... your local framer, art gallery director, art club secretary or art school teachers. If you show them samples of your work, and ask them for honest pricing advice, they will usually be willing to advise you.

Art shops, galleries, hotels, furniture stores, department stores and gift shops often buy, or will display paintings for sale, taking a modest commission.

Your local library, art shop and art gallery will usually have details of upcoming art exhibitions which you may be eligible to enter. There are lots of opportunities to exhibit and sell work... but above all else paint for your own pleasure and enjoyment. Exhibiting and selling work is a nice bonus when it happens.

Art clubs and art societies can be well worth joining. Libraries, art schools and newspapers will often be able to give you details of such groups. If you can't find a group ...Why not start one yourself?

Below. The joy of seeing your first works of art exhibited are beyond words. Don't forget you can also join your artist friends and colleagues in small local group exhibitions.

THE FLYING ARTIST'S GUIDE TO

SKETCHING

is one of a series of art books which introduce audiences of
all ages to the joy and beauty of artistic creation.

The first four titles in the series are:

The Flying Artist's guide to WATER CLOUR PAINTING
The Flying Artist's guide to OIL PAINTING
The Flying Artist's guide to PASTEL PAINTING
The Flying Artist's guide to SKETCHING

These titles can be ordered direct from:

Select Publications Ltd.
3918 Kitchener Street
Burnaby, BC Canada
V5C 3M2
Tel: (604) 415-2444
Fax: (604) 415-3444

Some helpful Do's and Don'ts

1. **Do** keep a pocket sketch book and pencil by you at all times.

2. **Do** try to spend 10-15 minutes every day sketching something around your home or work place.

3. **Do** turn the sketch upside down, or look at it in a mirror to check for errors before shading or painting it.

4. **Do** experiment sketching with different mediums, pencil, pen, charcoal, pastel... anything that makes a mark

5. **Do** go outside to sketch, as well as sketching indoors.

6. **Don't** forget to keep things simple, reduce things to basic shapes and build on the shapes.

7. **Don't** forget to take a camera with you if sketching outdoors; a sketch and a photo of the view can provide material for an original painting to be completed at home.

8. **Don't** forget to look after pencils, paper and your art materials. They will become faithful servants to your picture making.

9. **Don't** just sketch one view of a subject, try two or three sketches from different angles if possible.

10. **Don't** forget "ABS", Always Be Sketching.